Simply Science

ENERGY

Discover Science Through Facts and Fun

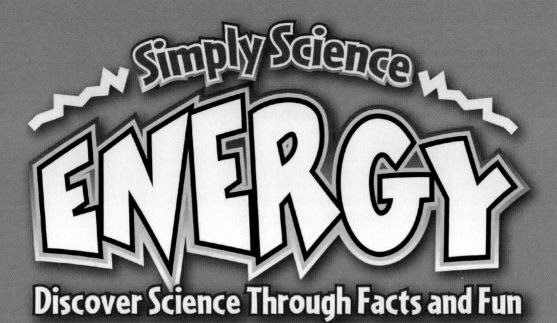

By Steve Way and Gerry Bailey

Science and curriculum consultant:
Debra Voege, M.A., science curriculum resource teacher

Gareth Stevens
Publishing

Please visit our web site at www.garethstevens.com.
For a free catalog describing our list of high-quality books, call 1-800-542-2595 (USA)
or 1-800-387-3178 (Canada). Our fax: 1-877-542-2596

Library of Congress Cataloging-in-Publication Data

Way, Steve.
     Energy/by Steve Way.
         p. cm.—(Simply Science)
     Includes bibliographical references and index.
     ISBN-10: 0-8368-9227-5   ISBN-13: 978-0-8368-9227-7 (lib. bdg.)
     1. Power resources—Juvenile literature. I. Title.
  TJ163.23.W378   2009
  621.042—dc   222008012398

This North American edition first published in 2009 by
Gareth Stevens Publishing
A Weekly Reader® Company
1 Reader's Digest Road
Pleasantville, NY 10570-7000 USA

This edition copyright © 2009 by Gareth Stevens, Inc. Original edition copyright © 2007 by
Diverta Publishing Ltd., First published in Great Britain by Diverta Publishing Ltd., London, UK.

Gareth Stevens Senior Managing Editor: Lisa M. Herrington
Gareth Stevens Creative Director: Lisa Donovan
Gareth Stevens Designer: Keith Plechaty
Gareth Stevens Associate Editor: Amanda Hudson
Special thanks to Mark Sachner

Photo Credits: Cover (tc) Soundsnaps/Shutterstock Inc., (bl) Roman Milert/Shutterstock Inc.;
p. 5 Keren Su/Corbis; p. 10 The British Library, all rights reserved; p. 12 (t) Gianni Tortolli/Science Photo
Library; (b) West Semitic Research/Dead Sea Scrolls Foundation/ Corbis; p. 13 (l) British Library/AKG-
Images, (tr) John Hedgecoe/TopFoto, (br) Randy Faris/Corbis; p.17 Newton Page/Shutterstock Inc.;
p. 18 Bettmann/Corbis; p. 21 (tl) Soundsnaps/Shutterstock Inc., (bl) R. Gino Santa Maria/Shutterstock
Inc., (bc) Lance Bellers/Shutterstock Inc., (br) Pure Digital 2006; pp. 22–23 Telepix/Alamy.; p. 24 Roman
Milert/Shutterstock; p. 25 Chris Cheadle/Stone/Getty Images; p. 26 Alejandro Bolivar/EPA/Corbis;
p. 27 Skyscan/ Science Photo Library.

Illustrations: Steve Boulter and Xact Studio

Diagrams: Ralph Pitchford

Printed in the United States of America

1 2 3 4 5 6 7 8 9 10 09 08

CONTENTS

What Is Energy?

Energy Helps Us Get Things Done!

Why do we need energy? To do things! Energy is the ability to do work. You used energy just to open the cover of this book!

Now your eyes are using energy to see the words you are reading. Your brain is using energy to figure out what the words say. If you have a light on so you can see the words more clearly, you're also using light energy.

If you are in a warm room, then you're using heat energy. So even reading a book uses all kinds of energy. In fact, we need energy to do everything.

Energy lets us do things, or it can be stored up so we can do these things later.

It takes energy to create heat.

What Is Power?

Power is the way we measure how much energy we're using each moment. It takes more muscle power to run up a hill instead of walking. Huff! Puff!

Energy can be found in many forms. Read on to learn all about them!

Pushing and Pulling

Energy and power can be seen
and used in many different ways.

1. human power

2. animal power

3. wind power

4. water power

5. solar power

6. burning energy

7. turning power

8. magnetic power

9. electrical power

10. nuclear power

Human Power

Humans need energy to move around, to think, and to keep our bodies alive and healthy. We get our energy from the food we eat.

Energy from food is used to keep our heart pumping, our lungs breathing, and our brain working. Energy from food also helps us grow and stay healthy. Each time we move, our muscles draw on this energy, too.

Energy Foods

Most of our food energy comes from carbohydrates. Foods like rice, pasta, potatoes, and bread contain lots of carbohydrates. We can also get energy from fats. Foods like cheese, cream, butter, and some meats contain fat.

Muscle Power

Our muscles need energy to move. We have two types of muscle. One type helps us carry out "fast action" exercise, such as sprinting. The other type of muscle helps us keep active for a longer time, such as when we run a marathon.

Pushing needs "slow" muscle action.

Fast or Slow?

Everyone has a different mix of these muscles. That's why some people are good at sprinting and some people are good at running marathons. Very few people are good at both sprinting and running long marathons!

Sprinting needs "fast" muscle action.

9

Animal Power

Throughout history, people have used animals to do work.

In many parts of the world, animals like horses and oxen help farmers plow fields so they can plant their crops.

Animals like camels and elephants are also used to help move people and other heavy objects.

Did You Know?

Sometimes people burn the dried dung of animals as fuel to keep themselves warm.

1. The leaf draws chemicals from the soil and energy from the Sun to help it grow.

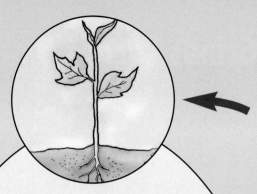

6. The soil is enriched by the bird's droppings and by the decaying eagle after it dies.

The Food Chain

Plants and animals pass energy along a **food chain**. Plants provide important food for animals but also draw food from the soil for themselves. **Decaying** dead animals and droppings from live animals all help enrich the soil.

Animals called **predators** eat other types of animals called **prey**. In this way, plants and animals all depend on each other for life and energy.

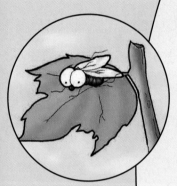

2. The fly eats the decaying leaf.

5. The eagle eats the snake.

3. The frog eats the fly.

4. The snake eats the frog.

Wind That Grinds Corn

1. Millstones were used for grinding corn into powder. They were heavy, and it took a lot of power to move them.

2. Early **millers** probably used the power of water to turn the grinding stones in their mills. Sometimes, though, the rivers ran dry. Then they had to find another source of energy to power the mills.

3. Horse power was used, but in time, a horse ran out of energy.

4. The millers needed an energy source that wouldn't run out or get tired. They knew that the wind powered boats. They wondered if they could use wind to power the mill, too.

5. Huge sails were attached to the outside of the mill. As the wind blew them around, the sails turned a pole. This, in turn, turned the grindstones, rotating them around and around and grinding the ears of corn to powder.

Wind Power

A windmill is a structure that uses the power of the wind to make energy.

A windmill uses sails that are driven around by the force of the wind. The first windmills were probably used to turn huge stone wheels. We use the power of the wind today. Modern windmills called wind turbines are used to make electric power.

If you made your own windmill out of a milk carton, your breath would be the energy source!

Water Power

The best source of water power comes from fast-moving water in rivers, rapids, or waterfalls. We call this kind of energy "kinetic energy," or energy of movement. It can be used to power machines.

A water wheel needs a force of water to move it. If the river runs dry, the wheel will not move.

The Water Wheel

The water wheel was invented more than 2,000 years ago. As water flows, it pushes against the blades of the wheel. Each blade is shaped like a shallow bucket. It scoops up water as the wheel rises and tips water out as it falls. The force of the moving water keeps the wheel turning.

The water wheel is often attached to the side of a mill. It is joined to machinery inside the mill by an axle. The turning water wheel turns the axle, and the turning axle powers the machinery.

- An overshot water wheel is turned by water falling from above.

- An undershot water wheel scoops rushing water from below.

Undershot water wheel

Water Power

It's amazing, but without the Moon in its **orbit** around Earth, our seas would not have waves or high and low **tides**!

The Moon is so big and so close to us that its **gravity** is able to pull Earth's seas slightly toward it. As Earth spins, the seas facing the Moon rise. Then, as Earth spins on, those same seas fall back again. The Moon's gravity is a powerful source of energy.

Turning Water Power into Energy

Have you ever been knocked over by a big wave? Then you know that waves have lots of energy in them. Scientists have been trying to find ways of turning some of that energy into electrical energy.

Floating Dams

One idea is to make a dam on the coast, or even lots of floating dams that fill up with water when the tide comes in.

tide flows in

When the tide goes out, the water passes through a machine called a generator that produces, or generates, electricity.

tide flows out

Pontoons

Another idea is to float objects called **pontoons** on the waves. As the pontoons bob up and down, their movement can be used to generate electrical energy. There aren't many wave pontoons in use yet. They disturb fish and birds that live in and around the sea.

pontoon

energy wave

Solar Power

All living things need the Sun's energy. Even in winter, the Sun keeps Earth warm enough for life. Heat from the Sun helps create wind and causes our weather. The Sun's heat and light give plants and animals energy to grow and move. The use of the Sun's light and heat energy is called solar power.

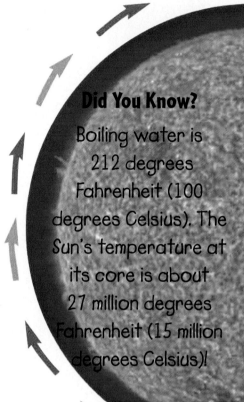

Did You Know?

Boiling water is 212 degrees Fahrenheit (100 degrees Celsius). The Sun's temperature at its core is about 27 million degrees Fahrenheit (15 million degrees Celsius)!

The Life-Giver!

The light energy produced by the Sun helps living things on Earth survive. It gives plants the energy they need to grow. It also helps our skin make its own vitamin D, which helps build strong bones.

Using the Sun's Energy

We can catch the Sun's light energy with solar panels. These panels are attached to the roof of a building like the one below. There, they catch energy that can be used to heat the building inside. The panels are painted black because dark colors absorb more energy from sunlight than lighter colors. Tubes of water pass through the solar panels. They get hotter and hotter and finally carry the heat to the inside of the building.

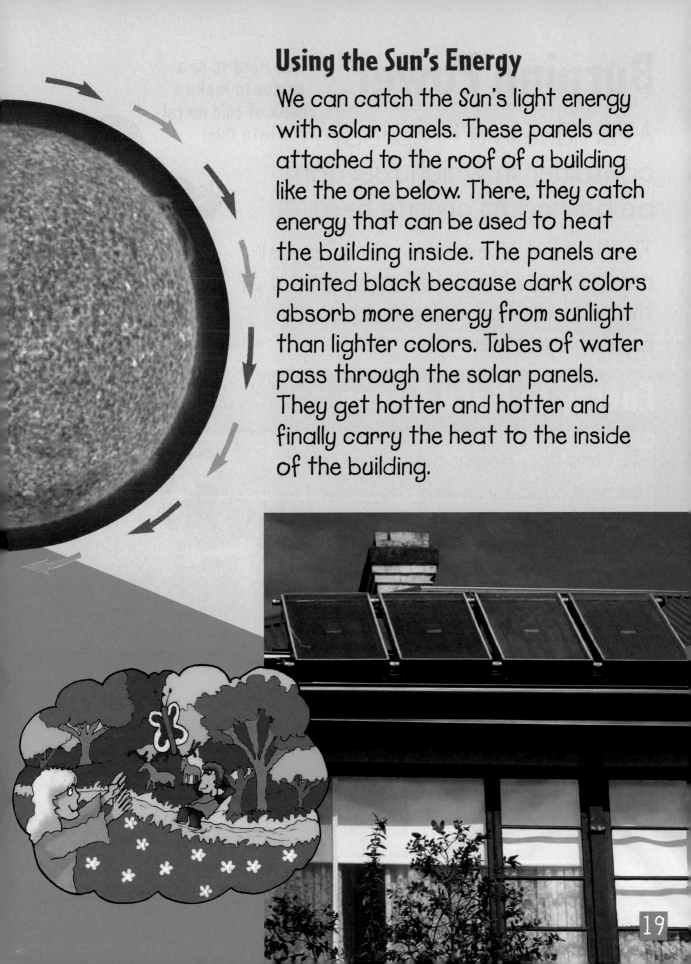

Burning Power

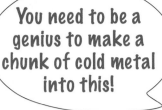

You need to be a genius to make a chunk of cold metal into this!

A furnace is a fireproof container in which fuel can be burned to create heat.

The first furnaces were probably just bowl-shaped fireplaces scraped out of the ground. Charcoal was a popular form of early fuel.

Energy to Make Armor

1. Long ago, people made iron metal by heating the iron **ore** they mined from the ground. The ore had to be made so hot that all the other metals in it were destroyed and only pure iron was left.

2. Early furnaces were small and used lots of charcoal. The worker fanned the flames to make the fire hot enough to melt iron.

Combustion

Combustion happens when a material, such as coal or wood, is set on fire. The material can only burn if the gas called oxygen is present. Combustion makes heat, light, and a waste product, ash.

3. Once the iron was melted, it needed to be kept hot. It had to stay soft and bendable so it could be made into tools. More and more charcoal had to be added, and the flames had to be fanned even harder.

4. Fires need the oxygen in the air to burn. The furnace owner knew the fire would burn brighter if it had more air blown around it.

5. A wind maker, called a bellows, was invented to do this job. We sometimes use these even today.

Turning Power

> I need a machine to fight my battles for me!

A catapult was a machine used in warfare to shoot heavy boulders.

Catapults were invented by the ancient Greeks. They were used until the 1500s as weapons to knock down the walls of enemy castles.

A Catapult Conquers a Castle

1. In ancient times, a castle was used as a place of shelter by villagers. It was also a house for the nobles and their soldiers. If the castle was attacked, soldiers could shoot from its walls. An army attacking a castle had to break down the walls.

2. Bows and arrows were no use when it came to doing this work. They were too lightweight.

Twisting Power

A catapult uses twisting force. Its rope is twisted tightly so it will uncurl once it is released. As it springs back into shape, it releases the arm of the catapult, and its heavy load is hurled into the air.

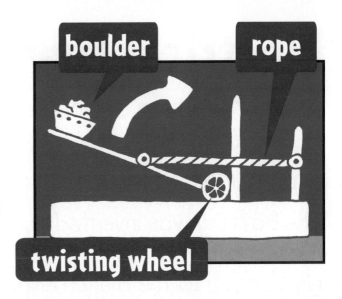

boulder

rope

twisting wheel

3. A machine was needed that would shoot a heavy weapon over the soldier's heads and hit the castle with force.

4. A huge boulder would be heavy enough to damage the castle wall, but what kind of machine could be used to throw it?

5. The answer was the catapult. A rope was wound tightly around a pole to make "twisting power." As the rope unwound, it created enough force to hurl boulders into the air.

Electrical Power

A battery is a storage device that is used to turn chemical energy into electrical power.

The battery was invented by Allessandro Volta. Volta presented his battery to the French emperor, Napoleon.

Let there be light!

A Store of Electric Power

1. Electricity is a kind of energy that is found all around us. We see it most clearly in the power that causes a flash of lightning.

3. He often saw people who had no coal or wood for fuel. He thought electricity could be a source of energy to help them stay warm.

2. Alessandro Volta knew that electricity was a strong source of light and heat. He wanted to invent a way to store it so that people could use it.

Batteries

A modern battery is usually made up of layers of chemicals inside a metal can. When the battery starts working, some of the chemicals "eat" at the metal container. These chemical changes to the can create an electric current.

A modern battery

4. It was easy to make small sparks of electricity by rubbing two stones together. Volta wanted to create a flow of electricity that would run like a continuous flow of water, however.

5. Volta decided to explore the energy in chemicals. This kind of energy is made by mixing metals and other materials together. He dipped the metals zinc and copper in salty water.

6. The reaction they made produced an electric current. Volta used his discovery to invent the first battery, a storehouse of electric power.

Energy That Powers a Motor

1. Michael Faraday was fascinated by electricity. He was also interested in magnetism, the power of certain metals to attract one another.

2. Faraday came from a poor family and didn't go to school. This didn't stop him from learning as much as he could.

3. The more he learned, the more he believed that magnetism and electricity were linked. He wanted to see if this was true.

5. By discovering that magnetism could help create an electric current, Faraday figured out how to keep the parts moving on what *became* the first electric motor!

4. He spun a piece of copper metal wrapped with wire between the two poles of a magnet and found that this created an electric current.

6. This was a simple discovery, but it changed the way people thought about electricity. Faraday used it to make a generator that could produce a flow of electric energy and create non-stop power for machines.

Magnetic Power

A bar magnet is a metal bar that has two ends. These are called its poles. One end is the south pole and the other the north pole. A magnet has the power to pull, or attract, many other metals to its surface.

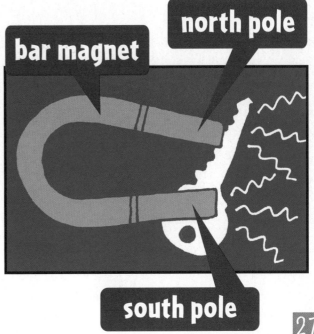

bar magnet

north pole

south pole

Nuclear Power

Every single thing on Earth, even air, is made up of tiny particles called atoms. Atoms are so tiny that scientists need powerful microscopes to see them. Even then, they can only see the biggest atoms.

Exploding an Atom

At the center of each tiny atom is its nucleus. In the nucleus are even tinier particles called neutrons and protons.

When a neutron hits a uranium atom, for example, it shatters that atom. This gives off lots of energy. We say that the uranium is "radioactive."

When energy is released by shattering an atom of either the metal uranium or plutonium, it can cause a **nuclear** explosion that is very powerful and dangerous!

a neutron

a nucleus is made up of neutrons and protons

Nuclear energy is produced at nuclear power stations. These power stations can produce a lot of energy from radioactive materials. These materials can be very dangerous, however. Nuclear energy has to be created very carefully to be safe.

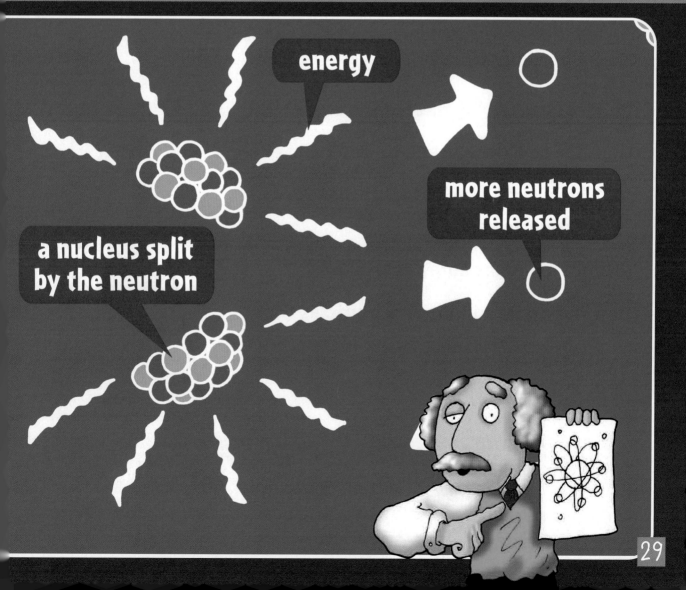

Energy Quiz

1. What gas is needed for combustion to happen?

2. Who invented the generator to make electricity using magnetism?

3. What did Allessandro Volta invent?

4. How long ago was the water wheel invented?

5. What can the Sun help us make in our skin that is good for our bones?

6. What causes the tides in the seas?

7. What do humans need to give them energy?

8. Who invented the catapult that used twisting power?

9. How hot is the core of the Sun?

10. What do we call the tiny particles that make up everything on our planet?

1. Oxygen 2. Michael Faraday 3. The battery 4. More than 2,000 years ago 5. Vitamin D 6. The Moon 7. Food 8. The ancient Greeks 9. 27 million degrees Fahrenheit (15 million degrees Celsius). 10. Atoms

Glossary

decaying: rotting, breaking down (as a dead plant or animal)

food chain: the relationship of plants and animals that shows who eats what and how energy is passed along from one plant or animal to another

gravity: the attraction, or pull, of one object on another, usually two very large bodies in space, such as Earth and its Moon

miller: person who operates a mill that grinds grain into flour

nuclear: having to do with the nucleus of an atom or with the energy that is released by the shattering of an atom

orbit: the path of a planet, moon, or other body in outer space as it circles another body

ore: a mineral in the ground that contains valuable metals or other substances in it

pontoons: floating objects that may be used to hold up a bridge or a dock

predators: animals that hunt or kill other animals for food

prey: an animal that is hunted or killed by another animal for food

tides: the rising and falling of the surface of oceans and seas as caused by the effects of the Moon's gravity on Earth

Index